Lost at the Fun Park

Story by Annette Smith
Illustrations by Paul Könye

Mom, Dad and Jonathan
went into the fun park.

"Look at the clown
on the big bike," said Jonathan.

"And look at the clown
with the balloons," said Mom.

"Dad, can we go for a ride
on the little boats?
Please, Dad," said Jonathan.

"Yes," said Dad.
"The little boats are fun.
I will go and get the tickets.
You stay here with Mom."

Dad came back with the tickets.

"Where is Jonathan?" he said.

"Jonathan went with you,"
said Mom.

"No," said Dad.

"Jonathan stayed here with you."

Jonathan ran up and down,
looking for Mom and Dad.

"Where is my mom?" he cried.
"Where is my dad?"

"Hello, little boy,"

said the clown with the balloons.

"Are you lost?"

"Yes," said Jonathan.

"I'm lost,

and my mom and dad

are lost, too."

"Who **are** you?" said the clown.

"I'm Jonathan Little,
  10 Hill Road," said Jonathan.

"Good boy, Jonathan,"
  said the clown with the bike.
"Stay here. Look at this!"

Mom and Dad saw the big balloon.

"Jonathan!" they shouted.

"Here I am!" shouted Jonathan.

"I'm going to stay with you,"

said Jonathan.

"I'm not going to get lost again."